Brilliant Support Activities

Understanding Light, Sound and Forces

Roy Purnell
Janet O'Neill,
Alan Jones

Brilliant
PUBLICATIONS

We hope you and your class enjoy using this book. Other books in the series include:

Understanding Living Things
printed ISBN: 978-1-78317-095-1
Ebook ISBN: 978-1-78317-099-9

Understanding Materials
printed ISBN: 978-1-78317-096-8
Ebook ISBN: 978-1-78317-100-2

Published by Brilliant Publications
Unit 10
Sparrow Hall Farm
Edlesborough
Dunstable
Bedfordshire
LU6 2ES, UK

E-mail: info@brilliantpublications.co.uk
Website: www.brilliantpublications.co.uk
Tel: 01525 222292

The name Brilliant Publications and the
logo are registered trademarks.

Written by Roy Purnell, Janet O'Neill and
Alan Jones

Designed and illustrated by Small World
Design

The authors are grateful to the staff and
pupils of Gellideg Junior School, Merthyr
Tydfil for their help.

© Text: Written by Roy Purnell, Janet
O'Neill and Alan Jones

Printed ISBN: 978-1-78317-097-5
Ebook ISBN: 978-1-78317-101-9

First printed and published in the UK in
2014

10 9 8 7 6 5 4 3 2 1

Contents

© Roy Purnell, Janet O'Neill and Alan Jones

Introduction to Everyday Physics

This book shows the relevance and importance of understanding the science of everyday physics. We are concentrating only on light, sound and forces including magnets and electricity, and introducing some aspects of weather.

It is NOT a complete textbook on all aspects of the area of Physics.

This series of three books is designed to help the slower learner, or any aged pupils with various learning difficulties operating at the lower levels of understanding of KS1 and KS2. The activities follow the guidelines of science concepts as outlined in the Programmes of Study for years 1–3 and selected topics of year 4 and year 5. The activities should help to develop the essential Scientific Enquiry skills as outlined in the National Curriculum, namely those of 'Observation', 'Predicting', 'Recording', and 'Drawing Conclusions' through the activities included in the book.

The books contain a mixture of paper-based tasks and also some 'hands on' activities. The following symbols on each sheet have been used to indicate the type of activities.

 What to do

 Think and do

 Read

 Investigate

The sheets involving practical investigations use materials readily available in most schools or homes. The activities have been vetted for safety, but as with any classroom based activity, it is the responsibility of the classroom teacher to do a risk assessment with their pupils in mind.

The sheets generally introduce one concept area per sheet. They are designed to be used by single pupils or as a classroom activity if all the pupils are working in the same ability range. Alternatively they can be used as a separate sheet for slower learners working on the same topic as the rest of the class, hence helping differentiation within the topic area. The sheets are easily modified for specific pupils or groups. They can be used in any suitable order as there is no hierarchy with the sequence in the books. They can be used with pupils in hospitals or experiencing long stays at home.

The sheets can be used for assessment purposes or homework tasks.

Generally the sheets can be used with older pupils if they are operating at levels expected of pupils operating within the expectations and understanding level commensurate with pupils at KS1 and KS2. The sheets use simple language and clear black line illustrations to make them easy to read without colour distractions. They have reduced number of words and a straightforward vocabulary to help poor readers or pupils whose language skills might be limited. Written responses are required so helping writing and communication skills of pupils. The completion of the sheets can be done by a support teacher responding to a verbal or a sign instruction by the pupil. It is essential that all pupils feel a sense of success and achievement when doing science as it is part of their everyday life.

No particular reference has been made to any specific type of learning difficulty or disability as the material has been successfully tested with a wide range of pupils. The teachers modify the method of use as the sheets can be enlarged or the instructions read onto a sound disc or computer. The sheets are easily converted to be shown on larger screens or computer screens.

The topics of this book match the New (and old) National Curriculum and cover the area of 'Everyday Physics' and help the pupils use the various processes and methods of science. The topics are arranged in groups matching the National Curriculum Programme of Studies.

The worksheets in this book sometimes overlap with other activities but this will help the pupils to grasp the concepts in a different context. Some topics also take ideas from another science area just to show the links between the everyday science we use. The worksheets can be used in any suitable sequence as this is not a logical teaching scheme. They are designed to give flexibility and diversity to teachers with pupils working with a wide range of abilities within a class. Some topics have been chosen that are from the POS of year 4 to 6 but written with the slower pupils in mind. Other topics can be linked with geography eg Rocks and minerals. Any numeracy work is at the lower levels of expectancy.

Some sheets encourage direct answers to specific questions whereas other activities require some degree of thinking before making a written response. The symbols on the sheets give an indication of this. The questions and presentation are simple but the level of pupil response can often reveal higher levels of understanding than expected.

National Curriculum POS and the Activities of this book
Because the New NC does not clearly indicate separate statements of the POS by using a nomenclature or numbering or letters within any areas it has been found convenient for OUR books to code and summarize these main sections of the NC. This will help the teacher see how the topics in this, and the other books in the series, cover the POS of the National Curriculum. All the relevant topics are covered, some more than once.

New National Curriclum 2014

Letter headings are ours but refer to the NC statements quoted on the pages of NC

Processes needing to be covered:	Content of the POS
KS1 Our Summary of POS which are appropriate for Pupils both in year 1 and year 2, 'Working Scientifically' (WS) page 139 of NC. WSa Asking questions, and answering WSb Observing and using simple equipment WSc Testing ideas WSd Identifying and Classifying WSe Using observations to suggest answers WSf Gathering data to answer questions	**KS1 Our Summary of POS for Year 1 'Everyday Physics', (P) pages 142–143 of NC** P1 Light Sources P2 Light and Shadows P3 Seasonal changes P4 Weather and seasons
Relevant Materials POS page 142 NC. KS1, year 1 M3 Simple Props of everyday materials M4 Comparing different materials M5 Changing shapes of solids M6 Identifying and comparing different materials M7 Comparing how things move on different surfaces	**KS1, Our Summary of POS for year 2 Everday Physics page 147 NC** P5 Sounds and hearing P6 Sounds near and far
Relevant Earth Science page 164 NC (year 5) E1 Movement of Earth and Planets E2 Movement of the Moon E3 Shape of sun, moon and Earth E4 Day and night	**Lower KS2 Our Summary of POS for year 3 and year 4 see page 153 NC** P7 Relected light P8 Size of shadows P9 to 13 All about magnets
	Years 3 and 4 Sound page 157 of NC P14 Sounds from vibrations P15 Pitch of sound P16 Volume of sound
	Year 4 Electricity page 158 of NC P17 Electrical appliances P18 Simple electric circuit P19 Simple series circuit P20 Switches P21 Conductors and insulators

Links to the National Curriculum

Activity Number	Title of Activity	NationalCurriculum Working Scientifically (WS)	National Curriculum POS for Everyday Physics (P)
	Light, Weather and the Earth		
9	How can we see things	a,b,c	P 1,2
10	Light makers	a,b,d,f	P 1,7
11	Shadows	a,c,d	P 2,8
12	Mirrors reflect light	a,b,c,e	P 7
13	Light words	c	P 1
14	Weather	a,b,c,d,e,f	P 3,4
15	Weather charts	a,b,c,d,e,f	P 3,4
16	The turning Earth	a,b,d	E 1,2
17	The Sun seems to move	a,b,c,e,f	E 1,4
18	Days, months, years	a,b,c,e	E 1,2,4
19	The seasons	a,b,c	P 4, E 3
20	The Earth, Sun and Moon	a,b,e	E 1,2,3
21	Space words	Wordsearch	
	Sounds		
22	Making sounds	a,c,e	P 5
23	Good vibrations	a,b,c,e	P 14,15
24	Sound passes through solids and gases	a,c,e	P 5,16
25	Pitch	a,b,c,d,e,f	P 14,15,16
26	Sound words	Wordsearch	
	Forces of Different Types		
27	Stretch and shape	a,b,c,e,f	P 9, M 5
28	The strong force of gravity	a,b,c, e,f	P 9
29	Air resistance	a,b,c,e,f	P 7
30	Forces can make things move	a,b,c,e	P 7, M 7
31	Balancing forces	a,b,e	P 9
32	Push and pull	a,b,c	P 9, M 7
33	Rough Stuff	a,b,c,e,f	P 9, M 7
34	Bungee jumping	a,c,d,e,f	P 9, M 7
35	Moving things	a,b,c,e	P 7,9
36	What do forces do?	a,b,c,e,f	P 9, M 7
37	Forces have a direction	a,b,c,e,f	P 9, M 7
38	Equal and opposite	a,b,c,e,f	P 9, M 7
39	Forces in muscles	a,b,c,e	P 9, B 6, B 21
40	Magnets	a,b,c,e,f	P 10,11,12

41	Magnets – push or pull?	a,b,c,e,f	P 10,12,13
42	Force words	Wordsearch	
	Electricity		
35	Useful electricity	a,b,c,d	P 17
36	Will the bulb light?	a,b,c,e	P 18,19,20
37	Try these circuits	a,b,c,e	P 18,19,20
38	Electricity – pass through or not?	a,b,c,e	P 21
39	How to dim bulbs	a,b,c,e	P 19,20
40	Dim or bright bulbs?	a,b,c,e	P 18,19,20
41	Switches	a,b,c,e	P 17
42	Electric words	Quiz	

How can we see things?

 ## Read

You can see something that gives out light, like a candle. The candle is called a **light**.

You can see anything that light bounces off, like a tree.

You cannot see when it is completely dark.

Mask

 # What to do

Draw light lines to show why Sam can see Jamie.

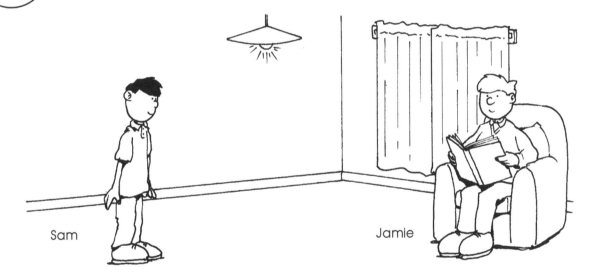

Sam

Jamie

Will the light pass through the wall? **Yes/No**

 # Think and do

Draw lines to show how Sam can see the light even when he's got his back to it.

light

Sam

mirror

Light makers

What to do

Put a tick ✓ by the things that **make** light.

Sun ☐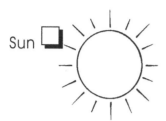

Dog ☐

Bulb that is on ☐

Cloud ☐

Fire ☐

Traffic lights ☐

Trees ☐

Television ☐

Mirror ☐

Candle ☐

Think and do

Make a list of all the different ways you can think of to light up a dark room.

. . . .

. . . .

. . . .

. . . .

. . . .

Shadows

Read

A shadow is made when light does not pass through an object.

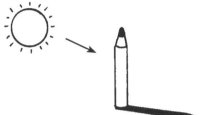

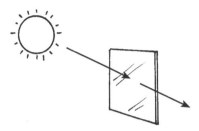

A pencil will make a shadow

Clear plastic or glass will not make a shadow. The light passes through.

What to do

Draw the shadow of the piece of card.

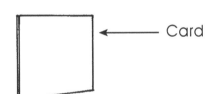

Card

Draw the shadow of the tree.

The shadow looks like the shape of the thing.

The shadow is made because the light is blocked off.

Think and do

Why does the shadow of a cat have the same shape as the cat?

. . . .

. . . .

Draw a picture to show its shadow.

Mirrors reflect light

Read

We see the pencil because the mirror reflects light back into our eyes.

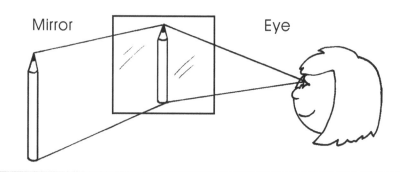

What to do

Draw where the mirror needs to be for you to see the pencil around a corner.

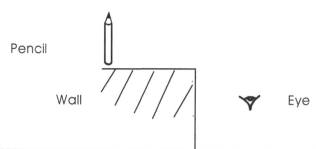

Draw two mirrors so that you can see the pencil.

The pencil is behind you. Where does the mirror need to go for you to see the pencil? Draw it.

What to do

Find the words that we use when we talk about light.

The words are listed underneath the grid.

z	s	h	i	n	e	t	r	e	d
o	q	i	n	d	i	g	o	r	s
r	j	r	e	f	l	e	c	t	s
a	x	y	z	g	h	j	z	w	h
n	y	e	l	l	o	w	d	b	a
g	v	w	w	x	j	d	g	l	d
e	h	n	m	p	q	r	z	u	o
z	v	i	o	l	e	t	z	e	w
g	r	e	e	n	q	r	w	r	s
e	y	e	z	m	i	r	r	o	r

shine   eye
shadow   red
reflect   orange
mirror   green
yellow   blue
indigo   violet

What to do

During the year, John had woken up to see these scenes when he looked out of the window.

Which season in the year was he looking at? Label and colour the pictures.

Spring   **Summer**   **Autumn**   **Winter**

. . . .

. . . .

Think and do

Complete the following sentences.

In Britain, ...

the hottest days are usually in . . . .

the coldest days are usually in . . . .

apples are usually ready for picking in . . . .

snow usually falls in . . . .

daffodils usually flower in . . . .

the day having the least daylight hours is in . . . .

the day having the most daylight hours is in . . . .

Weather charts

What to do

Make a weather chart for the year, similar to the one below.

Date	Time, usually midday	Describe the weather, or use drawings	Temperature outside	Season of the year

You can use any of the following words or draw a picture. You might need to use more than one word, for example, cloudy and sunny.

bright sun	**sunny**	**poor light**	**dark**	**gloomy**	**cloudy**
hot	**warm**	**heavy rain**	**cold**	**freezing**	**snowing**
dry	**windy**	**breezy**	**mild**	**light rain**	**misty**
foggy	**drizzle**				

Make up your own words for the weather today.

. . . .

. . . .

. . . .

Think and do

You could draw a graph showing the temperatures at noon for each day. This graph, when finished at the end of the year, will tell you if it has been a hot summer or cold winter.

You have made your own weather graph.

Try guessing the weather forecast for tomorrow and see if you are right.

The turning Earth

Read

We live on a planet called
Earth.

Look at the picture to see
where we live.

The Earth rotates around its axis
once in 24 hours (or 1 day).

In half a day the Earth turns
half the way round.

How many hours does this take
to go half way around?

. . . .

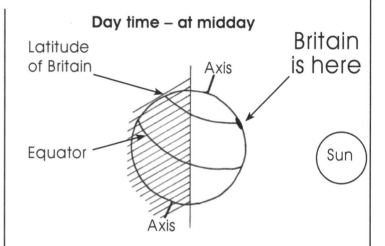

Day time – at midday

Latitude
of Britain

Axis

Britain
is here

Equator

Sun

Axis

Britain

Axis

Night time – at midnight

Axis

Latitude
of Britain

Sun

Equator

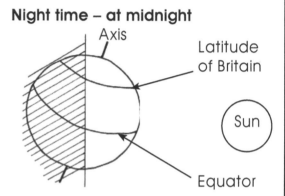

When we are facing the Sun, it is daytime.
When we are facing away from the Sun, it is
night time. Draw an arrow showing the
position of Britain at midnight on the night
time picture.

Think and do

Explain why it is cold at night.

. . . .

. . . .

What happens to the length of day and night
in the summer and winter?

. . . .

. . . .

© Roy Purnell, Janet O'Neill and Alan Jones

The Sun seems to move

Read

The Earth rotates. This makes it **seem** as though the Sun moves across the sky during the day.

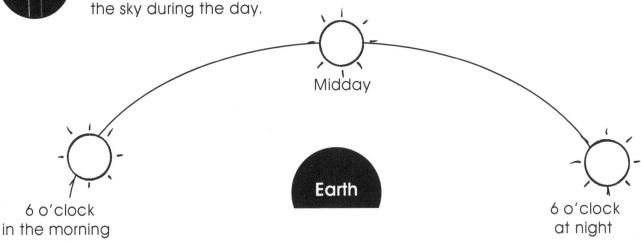

Midday

Earth

6 o'clock in the morning

6 o'clock at night

East

West

Put an **X** where the Sun will be at 9 o'clock in the morning.

Put a **Y** where the Sun will be at 3 o'clock in the afternoon.

What to do

The rotation of the Earth makes shadows move during the day.

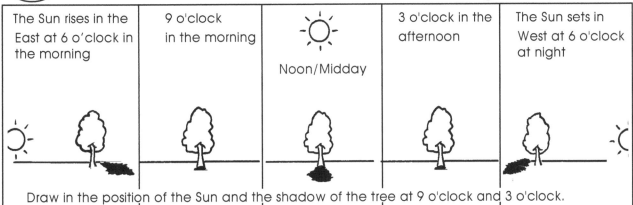

The Sun rises in the East at 6 o'clock in the morning	9 o'clock in the morning	Noon/Midday	3 o'clock in the afternoon	The Sun sets in West at 6 o'clock at night

Draw in the position of the Sun and the shadow of the tree at 9 o'clock and 3 o'clock.

Think and do

How can we use a sundial to tell time?

Days, months and years

Read

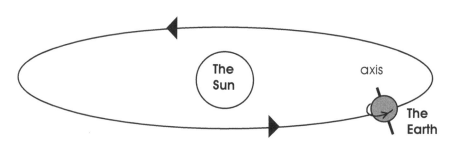

The Earth spins on its axis once a day.

The Earth rotates around the Sun once a year.

The Moon rotates around the Earth every 28 days.

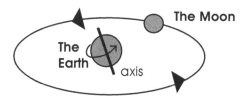

What to do

Answer these questions.

One rotation of the Earth around the Sun is called a . . . .

How many days are there in one year? . . . .

Each day the Earth completes one whole spin on its axis. How many times does it spin in one year? . . . .

How many days does it take the Moon to go around the Earth . . . .

Think and do

Which one of these is a **star**?
Which one of these is a **satellite** of the Earth?

The Sun is a . . . .

The Moon is a . . . .

The Earth is a **p** _ _ _ _ _ around the Sun

Do any other planets have moons? . . . .

. . . .

© Roy Purnell, Janet O'Neill and Alan Jones

The seasons

Read

The Earth spins once a day on its axis. The axis tilts so that in our summer the North pole is closer to the Sun and the South pole is further away.

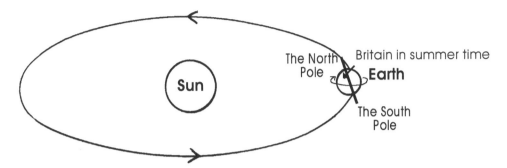

What to do

Draw on the diagram below, to show the position where the Earth would be if it were Spring, Summer, Autumn and Winter in Britain.

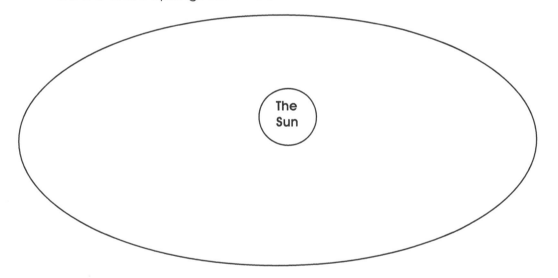

Think and do

Why is it colder in winter in Britain?

. . . .

Why is it winter in Australia when it is summer in Britain?

. . . .

. . . .

The Earth, Sun and Moon

 ## What to do

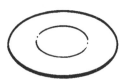

A plate

An orange

A box

The Earth, Moon and Sun are all the same shape as . . . .

Put a tick by the correct word.

The Earth moves around the   Sun ☐   Moon ☐

The Moon rotates around the   Sun ☐   Earth ☐

Planets, like Mars, move around the   Earth ☐   Moon ☐   Sun ☐

Label the diagram to show the Sun, Moon and Earth.

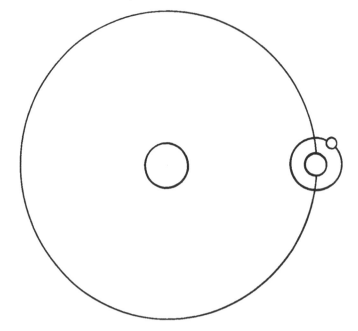

 ## Think and do
Put the planets Venus, Mercury and Mars on the diagram above

What to do

Find the words that we use when we talk about space and the sky. The words are listed underneath the grid.

s	x	e	a	r	t	h	a	e	g
k	k	s	t	a	r	d	s	m	r
y	o	v	k	v	o	t	t	n	k
o	f	q	s	a	d	w	r	z	i
k	h	g	u	s	a	p	o	o	u
e	e	w	n	m	i	v	n	f	m
t	g	x	a	b	l	c	a	x	o
d	p	l	a	n	e	t	u	k	o
s	p	a	c	e	a	b	t	z	n

sky

star

sun

moon

astronaut

space

planet

Making sounds

What to do

How can these things make sounds?
Use these words:

pluck	shake	tap
beat	blow	bang

Recorder

b _ _ _

Cymbals

b _ _ _

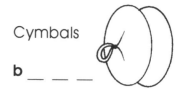

Rattle

s _ _ _ _

Triangle

t _ _

Guitar

p _ _ _ _ _

Drum

b _ _ _

Think and do

To make a louder sound with the drum you bang the drum
h _ _ _ _ _ _ .

To make a louder sound with the recorder you have to
b _ _ _ harder.

Brilliant Support Activities **Understanding Light, Sound and Forces**

© Roy Purnell, Janet O'Neill and Alan Jones

Good vibrations

What to do

Put some grains of rice on the skin of a drum.
Give the drum a few bangs.
What happens to the rice.

Did you notice the skin of the drum moving?   Yes ☐   No ☐

The drum skin **vibrates** up and down.

Investigate

Make this:

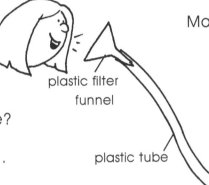

plastic filter funnel

Rice
Thin cling film

plastic tube   plastic filter funnel

Speak into the open end
quietly then loudly.

What happens to the grains of rice?

. . . .

What has caused the rice to move?

. . . .

Could you see the plastic **vibrating?**   Yes ☐ No ☐

This works a bit like a microphone.

Think and do

How can you alter the note a drum makes?

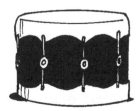

. . . .

What to do

A radio is playing loud music in the room next to your classroom.

You can hear the music in your room.

Use these words to complete the sentences:

air	wood	glass	window

The sound passes easily through the **a** . . . . in the rooms.

The sound passes less easily through the **g** . . . . in the windows.

The sound passes through the **w** . . . . frame.

The sound passes through the **w** . . . . in the floors and walls.

Think and do

Turn a radio on quietly. Put it in a cardboard box.

Can you still hear it?   Yes ☐   No ☐

Surround the radio with different materials. Find the best one to muffle the sound.

The best material to muffle the sound is . . . .

What to do

Three elastic bands are stretched and twanged. Which has the highest pitch? Tick the correct box.

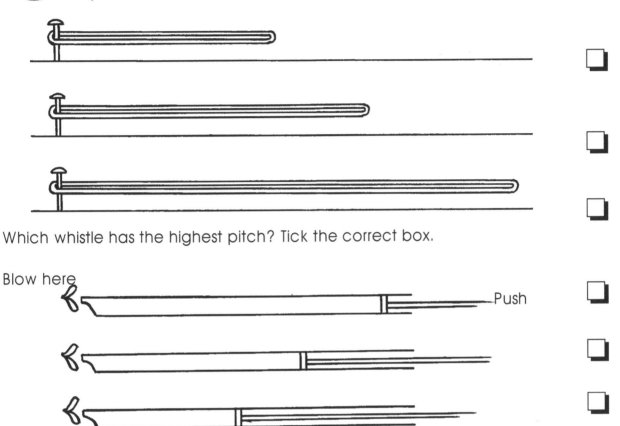

Which whistle has the highest pitch? Tick the correct box.

Blow here

Push

Which ruler will make the highest pitch when it is twanged? Tick the correct box.

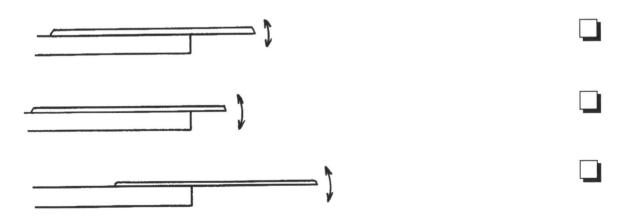

You can investigate this.

What to do
Rearrange the letters to make words we use when we talk about sound.

nesio

durm

olinvi

tremput

raguit

ludo

raiod

troomben

sotf

usicm

samarac

are

tlriaeng

scybmal

decorerr

piona

Brilliant Support Activities **Understanding Light, Sound and Forces**

© Roy Purnell, Janet O'Neill and Alan Jones

Stretch and shape

Read
Forces can make things change shape.

What to do
Draw or write what happens. Put a tick ✓ to show if it is a **stretch** or a **squash**.

	Draw here	Stretch	Squash
Hammer / Plasticine			
Exercise chest expander			
Soft cushion			
Bungee jumper			

Think and do
Look at this toy plane.

What happens to the elastic band when the propeller is wound up?

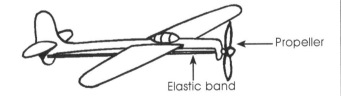

Propeller

Elastic band

. . . .

What happens to the elastic band when the plane flies?

. . . .

The strong force of gravity

Read

Gravity is a force. It pulls things towards the ground.

What to do

Two apples fall off the tree at the same time from the same height.

One apple is big and one is small.

Which will hit the ground first?. . . . .

When an apple falls off a tree, it is pulled down by the force of **g** . . . .

A man named Galileo dropped a big iron ball and a small iron ball from the top of a tall tower in Pisa, Italy.

Which one do you think hit the ground first?

. . . .

You can investigate this.

Use a marble and a metal ball bearing of the same size and drop them both at the same time onto a metal tray.
Listen to the 'clonk' as they hit the tray.
Did they land at the same time?

Think and do

Will the swing times be the same for both balls of Plasticine? They have the same length of string.

Time for 20 swings.

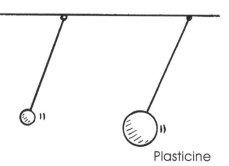

Plasticine

© Roy Purnell, Janet O'Neill and Alan Jones

Air resistance

What to do

The wind is helping Jo. Is it helping John?

John is . . . .

Direction of wind   Jo   John

How does Sharon use the air to move the boat?

. . . .

. . . .

. . . .

Direction of wind   Direction of Sharon ⟶

How does the boy on the parachute use the air?

. . . .

. . . .

. . . .

How does Tom use the air to make the kite fly?

. . . .

. . . .

. . . .

Think and do

How does a dandelion seed make use of the air?

How does the shape of the seed help?

Forces can make things move

What to do

List some **forces** in action in each of the pictures from the list.

magnetic   stretching   sliding   kicking   spinning

pulling   gravity   pushing

. . . .

. . . .

. . . .

. . . .

Think and do

What force acts to try to stop things moving?

F _ _ _ _ _ _ _ _

You can cut out the letters and rearrange them.

I	T	I	O	C	R	N	F

Balancing forces

Read

A seesaw balances when the force on one side equals the force on the other side.

Investigate

Make a seesaw with a rule and pencil. Make it balance by moving the coins.

Draw where the coins need to be to make the seesaw balance.

Coins

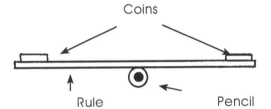

Rule   Pencil

Think and do

An adult who is twice the mass of a child uses a seesaw.

How can they make the seasaw balance?

Draw what happens now.

What to do

What is the name of the force Becky is using to move the trolley?

. . . .

What is the name of the force Becky is using to stop the trolley from moving?

. . . .

. . . .

The trolley is now full of shopping.
What do you think will happen if Becky lets go?

. . . .

. . . .

Think and do

Draw or write what will happen when Sam helps Becky. Show the direction of pushes and pulls.

© Roy Purnell, Janet O'Neill and Alan Jones

Rough stuff

Read

A moving car runs out of petrol and soon stops. The stopping force is called **friction** between the wheels and the road.

Investigate

How far does the toy car go? Try this yourself with a toy car.

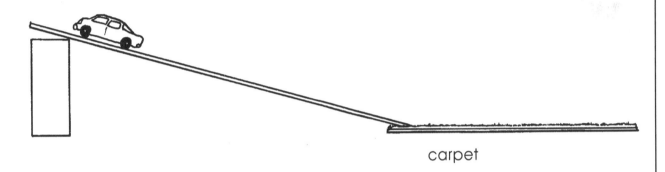

carpet

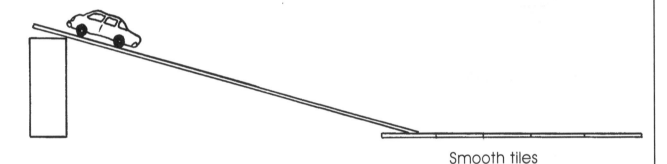

Smooth tiles

On which surface does the car go further? . . . .

A pram will move more easily on . . . . than on . . . . because

. . . .

Think and do

Give two reasons why roads are slightly rough.

1. . . . .

2. . . . .

What happens to moving cars when there is ice on the road?

. . . .

Bungee jumping

Read

Fred is a bungee jumper.
He is fixed by a thick elastic rope
to the top of a very high crane.

What to do

When Fred jumps, why is he not hurt?. . . . .

Why is the rope made of elastic and not ordinary rope?

. . . .

Use these words to complete the following sentences:

stretches	pulls	slows	gravity	longer

1. The rope **s** . . . . and gets **l** . . . . when Fred jumps.

2. When the rope stretches, it **s** . . . . down Fred's fall.

3. **G** . . . . pulls Fred downwards.

4. The stretch of the rope **p** . . . . Fred back upwards.

Think and do

Savita is twice as heavy as Fred.
What happens if Savita uses the
same bungee rope?

Bigger masses on the rope will stretch

the elastic rope   **more**   **less**

Tick the correct box.   ☐   ☐

© Roy Purnell, Janet O'Neill and Alan Jones

Moving things

What to do

Write **push** or **pull** to show what is happening in each picture.

How does James put on
his socks? . . . .

How does Sally move
the piano? . . . .

How does Marie move
the buggy? . . . .

How does Jack move the
zip down? . . . .

How does the horse move
the cart? . . . .

How does the man move
the car? . . . .

Think and do

Push or pull? Write the correct word.

1. How do we open a cupboard door? . . . .

2. How do we put on trousers? . . . .

3. Rugby players in a scrum? . . . .

What do forces do?

Read

You cannot see a force, but you can see what a force does.

What to do

Forces are being used in these pictures.
Show the direction of the forces.

Squeezing an orange

Magnet and paper clips

Stopping a bike

Someone skipping

Kicking a football

Ironing clothes

Think and do

What force makes the child slide down the slide?

. . . .

How does the child stop at the bottom?

. . . .

Forces have direction

Read

The force of the wind can move a sailing boat forward.
The arrow shows the direction of the force.

Force of wind ⟶

What to do

Draw arrows on the pictures to show the direction of the forces.

Man pushing buggy

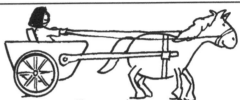

Horse pulling cart

Girl moving sledge

Woman pushing car

Boy pulling fish from water

Wind blowing tree

Bird pulling worm from the ground

Dog pulling tablecloth

Think and do

Mary lifts her heavy school bag off the floor.

Draw a picture to show what she does.

Draw arrows to show the direction of the force she uses.

Equal and opposite

Read

Two tug of war teams pull in opposite directions.

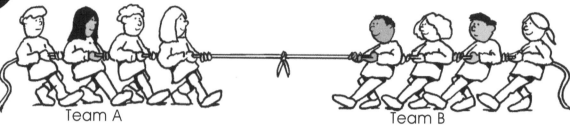

Team A   Team B

When the two forces are the same, the teams do not move.
Team A is working against Team B.

What to do

Team A gets an extra person. Write or draw what happens.

Use these words to complete the sentences.

same   **opposite**

Forces can help each other if they are going in the . . . . direction.

Forces can balance out each other if they are going in the . . . . direction.

Think and do

Draw in the direction of the force
when picking up the bucket.

Brilliant Support Activities **Understanding Light, Sound and Forces**

© Roy Purnell, Janet O'Neill and Alan Jones

Forces in muscles

What to do
Look at the pictures of muscles working.
Draw arrows to show the direction of the force by the muscles.

Think and do
What muscles do you use when on a trampoline? Draw a picture.

Magnets

Read

A magnet can pick up iron paper clips.
When it does this, the attractive force of the
magnet is stronger than the force of gravity.

Investigate

There are several shapes of magnet:

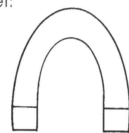

Bar   Horse shoe   Ring magnet

One end is called the **North pole**.

The other end is called the **South pole**

Is the attractive force the same at both ends?

Use iron paper clips to investigate this.

Think and do

Where are magnets used in the home?

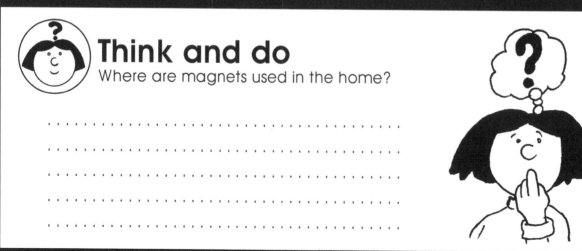

. . . .

. . . .

. . . .

. . . .

. . . .

Magnets – push or pull?

Investigate

Use some magnets to try this.
First predict if they will **repel** (push away) or **attract** (pull together).

	My prediction	What happened?
Put two different ends of a magnet close to each other. N S N S		
Put the same ends of two magnets together. N S S N		
Put one magnet on top of the other, matching the colours. N S / N S		

What to do

Use **North** or **South** to complete the sentences:
A . . . . pole attracts a South pole.
A North pole repels a . . . . pole.
A south pole repels a . . . . pole.

Think and do

A compass is a magnetic pointer needle on a pin.
The pointer can move about freely.

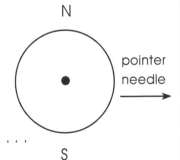

Draw the pointer on the compass shape pointing north.
What is attratcing the needle? . . . .
. . . .

Force words

What to do

Put a tick ✓ by the words that we use when describing a **force**.

gravity ☐   pull ☐   sheep ☐   zebra ☐

push ☐   radio ☐   squeeze ☐   mat ☐

change shape ☐   food ☐   start ☐   spring ☐

stopping ☐   window ☐   apple ☐   braking ☐

change direction ☐   moving ☐   elastic ☐

stretch ☐   orange ☐   friction ☐   classroom ☐

spring balance ☐   paper ☐   shove ☐   pencil ☐

speed ☐   lifting ☐   fall ☐   run ☐

Read

Electricity comes from batteries or power stations. We call electricity from power stations **mains electricity.**

What to do

Use these words to complete the sentences.

 bulb

 kettle

 washing machine

 calculator

 mobile phone

 television

 radio

1. A r. . . . . needs electricity.

2. A b. . . . . uses electricity to make light.

3. A t. . . . . needs electricity to give a picture.

4. A w. . . . . m. . . . . uses electricity to get clothes clean.

5. A k. . . . . boils water using electricity.

6. A m. . . . . p. . . . . gets its energy from a b. . . . .

7. A c. . . . . uses electricity to do sums.

Think and do

Find one new thing that uses a battery for electricity.
Find one new thing that uses mains electricity.

Write a sentence about each one.

Will the bulb light?

Read

For a bulb to light you **must** have a complete circuit. The electricity must go from the battery, through the wire, through the bulb and back to the battery.

What to do

Trace the path of the electricity with your finger.
You can investigate this if you wish.

Will the bulb light?

Yes ☐   No ☐

Will the bulb light?

Yes ☐   No ☐

Will the bulb light?

Yes ☐   No ☐

Will the bulb light?

Yes ☐   No ☐

Think and do

Draw in the wires to
make the bulb light.

 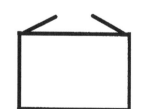

© Roy Purnell, Janet O'Neill and Alan Jones

What to do

Look at the pictures. Predict if the bulbs will light.
Make the circuits using wires, bulb and battery, and see if you were correct.

	My prediction	What happened?
	On/Off	On/Off
	On/Off	On/Off
	On/Of	On/Off
	On/Off	On/Off
	On/Off	On/Off

Think and do

Draw a circuit with three bulbs. Make sure all three bulbs will light.

Electricity – pass through or not?

Read

Electricity passes through metal.
It does not pass easily through plastic, wood, brick or concrete.

What to do

Look at the pictures. Predict which things
will let electricity pass through. Make a circuit.
Add each thing to the circuit in the gap and see if you were correct.

	My prediction	What happened
Drawing pin or nail	On/Off	On/Off
Plastic spoon	On/Off	On/Off
Metal spoon	On/Of	On/Off
Piece of wood	On/Off	On/Off
Coin	On/Off	On/Off
Pebble or stone	On/Off	On/Off

Think and do

Things that let electricity pass through are called **conductors.**

Why are metal electric wires covered with plastic?

. . . .

How to dim bulbs

Read

Batteries push electricity around circuits through wires and bulbs. It is harder to push electricity through bulbs than through wires. That's why the bulb glows and gets warm.

Bright

Dim

One bulb, bright

Two bulbs, dim

 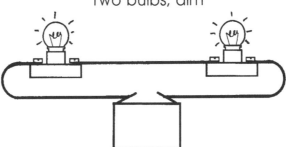

It is harder to push electricity through very long wires than through short wires.

Short wire, bright

Very long wire, dim

 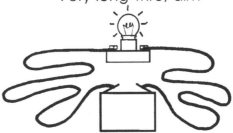

What to do

1. In which circuit will the bulb be **brightest A, B** or **C**?   Answer ☐

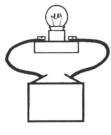

A   B   C

2. In which circuit will the bulb be **dimmest   D** or **E**?   Answer ☐

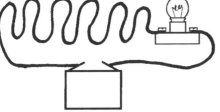 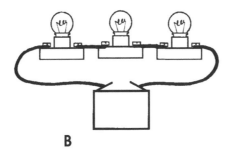 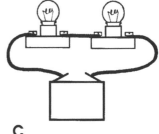

D   E

Dim or bright bulbs?

Read

Batteries push electricity around a circuit.
When two batteries are joined in a circuit, the push is twice as strong. Then the bulb is brighter.

Bright

Dim

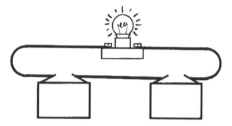 

Two batteries and two bulbs will have the same brightness as one bulb and one battery

Three bulbs and three batteries will be brighter than two batteries and three bulbs.

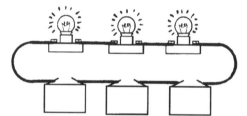 

What to do

Look at these circuits:

In which one are the bulbs the brightest? . . . .

In which one are the bulbs the least bright? . . . .

A   **B**   **C**

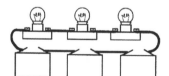
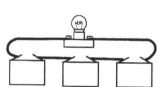

What to do

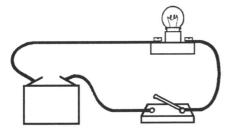

What happens to the bulb when the switch is closed?

. . . .

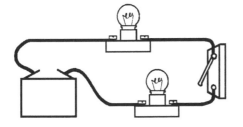

What happens to the bulbs when the switch is closed?

. . . .

. . . .

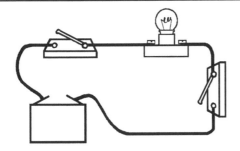

What happens when both switches are closed?

. . . .

What happens when one switch is closed? . . . .

. . . .

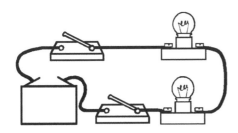

What happens when both switches are closed?

. . . .

What happens when one switch is closed?. . . . .

. . . .

Think and do

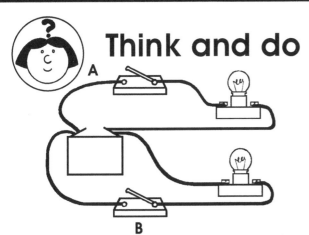

What happens when switch **A** is closed?

. . . .

What happens when both **A** and **B** switches are closed?

. . . .

Electric words

What to do

Put a tick ✓ by the things that need electricity to work.

sheep ☐   bulb ☐   tree ☐   Christmas lights ☐

flower ☐   wire ☐   cat ☐   underground train ☐

motor ☐   lollipop ☐   television ☐   wall ☐

switch ☐   bread ☐   radio ☐   road ☐

doorbell ☐   door ☐   refrigerator ☐

torch ☐   computer ☐   street light ☐

cable ☐   headlight ☐   dog ☐

circuit ☐   vacuum cleaner ☐   coal fire ☐

battery ☐   traffic lights ☐   book ☐

Brilliant Support Activities **Understanding Light, Sound and Forces**

© Roy Purnell, Janet O'Neill and Alan Jones

Lightning Source UK Ltd.
Milton Keynes UK
UKOW07f0821130116

266309UK00004B/48/P